MEDITATING

ON

FOUR QUARTETS

Excerpts from FOUR QUARTETS by T.S. Eliot
are reprinted by permission of Harcourt Brace
Jovanovich, Inc.; copyright 1943 by T.S. Eliot;
renewed 1971 by Esme Valerie Eliot.

International Standard Book No.: 0-936384-15-8
Library of Congress Catalog No.: 83-72285

Published in the United States of America
by Cowley Publications.

Cover design by James Madden, SSJE.

MEDITATING

ON

FOUR QUARTETS

JOHN BOOTY

Cowley Publications

EDITOR'S NOTE

In order to read John Booty's meditative and devotional essay on T.S. Eliot's long poem, we recommend that you keep a complete text of the *Four Quartets* close by. It was not possible for us, of course, to reproduce the entire poem and the structure of Booty's essay does follow that of the text throughout. A substantial number of quotations from the *Quartets* do appear, however, in order to highlight different sections of the poem and to guide the reader on. We suggest you use the small paperbound edition of *Four Quartets* issued by Harcourt Brace, which is excellent for making notes, or the text in *The Complete Poems and Plays.*

CLS

i. INTRODUCTION

T.S. Eliot's *Four Quartets* has become a classic in the tradition of western spirituality and of Anglican spirituality in particular. There is a growing multitude of those who have read and continue to read these poems for the ways in which they nurture the spirit. The reasons for their influence are many. For one, Eliot, for all his sophistication and elitism, is a vivid example of the many educated moderns in the West who suffer the tortures of the damned as they struggle to live in what Auden has called "the Age of Anxiety." Fear of death and guilt for sin pale beside the anxiety aroused by the threat of meaningless that dominates our times. In various writings, from *The Waste Land* on, Eliot has portrayed with telling effect the modern dilemma – the horror infecting the very core of humanity. The horror of meaningless existence, empty and indifferent, sometimes disguised by busyness or the twittering of such as the aunts and uncles of *The Family Reunion*, is most vividly portrayed in "The Fire Sermon" of *The Waste Land* where the typist submits to the sexual assault of the sailor and when it is over, dismisses the whole episode with a yawning indifference, "hardly aware of her departed lover."

Time and again Eliot makes contact in his poetry with our inner selves, spirit touching spirit, revealing our predicament as humans in a world indifferent to the deepest human relationships and to God who gives life in life-giving relationships. Eliot sees it all, feels it all so keenly, because the man of anxiety is also – howbeit tremulously – a man of faith. Having made contact with us where we are, teetering on the verge of the abyss, the poet leads us, gently, using sparingly the traditional, time-worn and thus some-times seemingly outmoded language of the Bible and theology. He leads us forward by helping us acknowledge the revelation that beyond meaninglessness and the abyss there is meaning and life, new and everlasting. Using all of the poetic craft at his command, this modern poet testifies to the reality of the Christian gospel and over and over again tells us that we by ourselves cannot make our present existence meaningful. We must be still, letting our minds

1

and hearts open up to receive the meaning from beyond ourselves, from eternity. Humility, in this context, is not just a virtue, it is the greatest virtue.

Once having received the meaning, perceiving the pattern whereby the chaos is ordered, we then see, and hear, and understand the true nature of each life and of the cosmos. Our seeing and hearing is, then, beyond our wildest expectations. We enter upon the way of faith, the faith which breeds hope and love. Two points must be made at this juncture. The revelation is received in time. There is no escape from the present. Time is intersected by eternity only in time. The Incarnation is the key to this understanding. Thus we live in the midst of contradictions, ambiguities, and conflict — the chaos of this age — but we live now, having received the meaning of all, in faith. All opposites are comprehended in that which faith receives, producing for individuals and for society reconciliation, wholeness, harmony — the music of the spheres.

The second point that must be made is that the revelation occurs through a person, the Logos, named Christ Jesus the Incarnate, and his body the Church. Natural human beings without faith in Christ occasionally catch glimpses of ultimate meaning and have visions of the wholeness beyond the chaos. Christians on the other hand live within the context of unifying meaning in the Church, the Church liturgy, word and sacrament, and the thought and activity that proceeds from those graceful gifts. The regular, although not constant or uniformly intense, awareness of the divine illumines the darkness of this present time.

These poems are also Anglican, partaking of the somewhat elusive Anglican ethos. They are Anglican not only because they were written by a devout Anglican High Churchman, but because of what they emphasize. Eliot affirmed the tradition of Richard Hooker and Lancelot Andrewes, a tradition that is grounded in the Christian faith, sure of what it professes, partaking of the order that dominated culture before the emergence of the modern era. The tradition is also imbued with a breath of culture that causes those who profess it to embrace the truth as found in nature as well as in the Christian gospel, believing as Hooker believed that

2

grace presupposes nature, Scripture the law of nature, and that the moral law of reason is operative, although crippled, in all of human existence, Christian or not.

In the sixteenth and seventeenth centuries that tradition located the intersection of time and eternity, the meeting of nature and grace, in the Incarnation of Jesus Christ, but it did not forget the Cross. Indeed, the tradition holds the conviction that the Incarnation is known on account of the Cross, but also that the Cross is finally comprehensible to people in time by virtue of the Incarnation. Eliot is a faithful participant in this tradition. He is also an inheritor of the modification of the tradition that occurred, as a result of the Oxford Movement of the nineteenth century. As an Anglo-Catholic he was devoted to Mary, "the daughter of her Son." He was deeply appreciative of late medieval mysticism and of mysticism in general, possessed a strong attachment to the Eucharist, in Tractarian terms, advocated spiritual discipline, and went regularly to confession. And he revered Dante. The *Four Quartets* are in consequence Anglican, a modern classic of Anglican spirituality.

Many people reading the poems over and over again have testified to the belief that through reading them they have glimpsed the divine and have been refreshed in the spirit. It is my hope that as you read this interpretation of the *Four Quartets* you begin to be aware — if you are not already aware — of the wealth of inspiration these poems contain. I write as a devotee, having heard Eliot read these poems on the radio in the 1940's and having read them repeatedly myself. Let me recommend that those unfamiliar with the poems either read them through aloud once, without pausing to understand all that the poet says, listening to the music of them, or else listen to Eliot read them on the recording still generally available. Having done that you are ready to read them more slowly, pondering individual poems, lines here and there, meditating upon this phrase or that word, beginning over again, using commentaries such as this interpretation and works mentioned in the notes at the end of this essay. The point is that to read these poems as they should be read they must be approached in humility, with openness, and with expectation.

3

Reading thus you shall better hear the music reflecting the music of the spheres and shall know what Eliot means when he writes:

> The music of a word is, so to speak, at a point of intersection: it arises from its relation first to the words immediately preceding and following it, and indefinitely to the rest of its context; and from another relation, that of its immediate meaning in that context to all the other meanings which it has had in other contexts, to its greater or less wealth of association. (*Music of Poetry*)

T.S. Eliot's *Four Quartets* can be viewed from a number of different perspectives: aesthetic, poetic, theological, philosophical, musical, historical, and political. All have their validity and all can be illuminating, but at the same time such perspectives are partial and tend to distort the poems taken as a whole. The poems can also be studied in relation to the influences impinging upon the poet's life and thought. For instance, the prewar movement in abstract art known as Vorticism, with its whirlpool of energy metamorphosed into form, form that is still and still moving, seemingly influenced the speculations of "Burnt Norton." The influence of French Symbolism is also evident throughout the poems. Stéphane Mallarmé was the symbolist who had the greatest influence on Eliot's work; he suggested that the ideas contained in his own poems were not to be apprehended by reason, but rather through poetic intuition. Only thus, Mallarmé believed, can the ideal be known. Symbols, through verbal music, typography, and pattern evoke, as far as possible, that which otherwise eludes expression: the aesthetic and the metaphysical ideal. Of Mallarmé, Steffan Bergsten remarks that he was among the first to write "discontinuous or disconnected poetry — that is, poetry which rejects the usual means of ensuring the continuity of idea essential to the poem, if it is to have the unity of a great work of art."[1]

4

The necessary unity, for Mallarmé and others of the same mind, was not to be based on "obvious emotional association, the facile metaphor, the patent sequence of events, cause and effect," but rather on the images that superficially disconnected and dissociated words and phrases suggest, images that evoke experiences and feelings. These are feelings and experiences, Bergsten goes on to say, which "correspond closely to those in the poet's mind, and not necessarily in his life."

There are also philosophical influences evident in these poems. The paradoxes of Vorticism were anticipated many centuries earlier by Heraclitus, the sixth-century Greek philosopher. For instance, we find in "Burnt Norton" the dictum, "The way upward and the way downward are one and the same." This amazing statement is cited by Eliot at the beginning of the *Four Quartets*. The other Heraclitean dictum, "Although the Word (*logos*) is common (universal), the many (most people) live as though they possessed a wisdom of their own," points toward the metaphysical ideal and argues in a way deeply embedded in Eliot's mind that there is an order, a wholeness, a harmony beyond the apparent chaos of everyday experience. Putting the two citations together, Heraclitus seems to have said that the order — the harmonious pattern — precedes the chaos and, further, is that by which and in which we perceive that opposites are not eternally separate but are different aspects of the whole, and are therefore capable of being reunited in some fashion. Indeed, in that pattern the opposites — the paradoxes — are resolved, the many being comprehended in the One.

Eliot need not have received this wisdom from F.H. Bradley, the British Idealist on whose philosophical teachings he wrote his doctoral dissertation, but it seems likely that Bradley, along with the influence of Vorticism, French Symbolism, and the Heraclitean world view, helped him to arrive at the metaphysic that dominates the *Four Quartets*. For Bradley, and for Eliot, reality (and thus truth) is an unanalyzable and unified whole, much like the Logos of Heraclitus. This metaphysical statement stands in direct opposition to the empiricist conviction that reality consists of discreet facts and events, each independent of all others. As Richard Wollheim puts it,

5

We think on the assumption that the world is like a vast jig-saw puzzle which can be taken to bits and studied fragmentarily, whereas, in fact, it is more like a work of art whose point, whose life, whose existence depends on being taken whole, on being seen as one.[2]

How do we come into contact with this reality described as the unanalyzable and unified whole? By means of a process of knowing that is prior to thought, for thinking involves analysis into parts and so results in the destruction of the unified whole. This knowing, which is prior to thought, F.H. Bradley calls "immediate experience." It is Mallarmé's poetic intuition, the "feeling" described by other Symbolists and used by Bradley himself as a definition of immediate experience, and it is the "unified sensibility" of the metaphysical poets, of Herbert, Donne, Vaughan, and Crashaw. It is important not to identify such feeling with consciousness, for consciousness belongs to a latter stage of knowing. "Immediate experience" is feeling prior to consciousness, and so it is without object or subject.

To put it another way, "Time is a 'felt whole' in which there are moments of knowledge:

> the moment in the rose-garden,
> The moment in the arbour where the rain beat,
> The moment in the draughty church at smokefall. . . ."[3]

These are moments in which past and present and future are comprehended and relate us to the still point, which is also a point of view that interprets all of existence. In such moments we glimpse eternity—the reconciliation of opposites, real and ideal. Such moments find meaning only in memory, which unites past and future, so that passing moments in time can be contemplated in their eternity.

Four Quartets is concerned with the apprehension of the whole, beyond the apparent chaos of opposites and paradoxes. In addition, these poems are concerned with providing the poet and the reader with an experience of that reality which is the

6

unanalyzable whole. In order to do this Eliot does not seek to express the truth, or reality, for this is impossible. The poet can only try to indicate reality by indicating experiences and points in time where truth reveals itself. Truth reveals itself in the patterns of human events rather than in isolated episodes, events which cohere and mutually reinforce. "The form of *Four Quartets*," writes one critic, "symbolizes this belief, for they establish their meaning not by statement, nor by logical progression, but by musical structure, a coherence which transcends both. . . ."[4] Or we may say that the meaning is apprehended not by analysis of discreet words and phrases, but rather by the experience of words interacting to reach beyond their own individual symbolic content to evoke a meaning that is perceived by the reader as a discovery— an amazing surprise.

Eliot's metaphysical perspective was influenced by much else. He was deeply influenced by Dante's *Divine Comedy* with its poetic purity, emotional range, and its allegorical levels of meaning. He read widely in the metaphysical poets of seventeenth-century England with their unified sensibility, their understanding of order and of pattern, and their struggles to express what they experienced intuitively. Eliot was also influenced by the mystics, and in particular St. John of the Cross and Julian of Norwich, with their poetic expression of the wholeness beyond the chaos of everyday existence. Also there was Eliot's own experience.

A keenly sensitive man, he was only too aware of the tragic incompleteness of his own life. It is not possible for us to ignore the impact upon the poet and his craft made by the death of his friend Jean Verdenal in the mud of Gallipoli, which was followed the next month by Eliot's precipitous and tragic marriage to Vivien Haigh-Wood. This marriage occasioned a predictable emotional and spiritual breakdown and eventually ended, in 1933, with legal separation and divorce from his wife. Such deeply personal and private pain influenced Eliot's perception of existence and reality at all levels. So, too, the events of public life in England, from the giddy Twenties through the ominous Thirties to the horrors of the Second World War, stand in the background and are sometimes openly acknowledged by the poet in his poems.

To read the last three of the *Four Quartets* is to be reminded, time and again, of the trials through which Britain and Eliot went during the 1940's. Such personal and historical details serve to emphasize further, but do not seriously challenge, the fact that the *Four Quartets* have to do with the quest for a unified and unanalyzable whole. They represent a search for a reality that provides meaning and hope, which is also the quest to transmit the meaning and the hope in such a way that both poet and reader experience saving wholeness through the words, the shapes, the images, and the music of the poems.

ii. BURNT NORTON

One afternoon, it may have been in 1934, Eliot went with Emily Hale, an American friend, to visit the house and garden of Burnt Norton at the edge of the Cotswolds in Gloucestershire. It was a quiet, remote place with a view of the Vale of Evesham and the Malvern Hills in the distance. There Eliot discovered a rose garden and, through a hedge, a drained pool. These are the images which recur in the first movement of "Burnt Norton." Of this experience Helen Gardner writes, "The garden, in the stillness and beauty and strange remoteness from the world, stirred in Eliot profound memories and brought together disparate experiences and literary echoes."[5]

Concerned for remembrance of things past, Eliot begins "Burnt Norton" with a meditation on time reminiscent of St. Augustine in the eleventh chapter of his *Confessions*. Emotionally intense memories of the past, evoked by his present experience in the garden, influence Eliot's perception of the future. This is a commonplace occurrence. But as he reflects on the ordinary human experience of time, Eliot also has in mind the conviction, widely held, that past-present-future are the eternal Now for God. And if this conviction is true, then it would seem that all is predetermined and speculation about what might have been is pointless, even idiotic. The Christian viewpoint is expressed in Eliot's play, *Murder in the Cathedral*, where the poet explains that all are fixed in an "eternal action," to which all give their willed consent. The *Quartets*, however, represent a different stage. The poet of the *Quartets*, says Moynihan, "cannot yet will his predetermined part in the fixed timelessness of God. What kinds of things the speaker thinks and what he feels as he seeks to consent, seeks to will his part in the eternal action, are the matter of the *Quartets*."[6]

After his brief meditation on time, Eliot directs his readers to look back and discover in memory that first world of childhood experience. What we find when we do look back is an illusion ("deception"), for what we remember has more to do with who we are now than who we were or might have been. Indeed, the "we" that we are may also be the "they" who accompany us, alter egos involving self-deception, or figures like the Eumenides, the furies of the *Family Reunion* or, more certainly, what Helen Gardner characterizes as 'the grownups,' who provide the secure and loving background for the children's play.[7]

There in the rose garden, in a magical, mystical moment of intense if illusory consciousness, while looking down into the dry pool, the timeless is encountered. With caution Eliot might speak of an immediate experience of the unified whole: "And the pool was filled with water out of sunlight,/ And the lotos [Buddha's lotos, symbol of contemplation and love] rose, quietly, quietly,/ The surface glittered out of heart of light." And the Eumenides or furies, parents, other selves, "they," stand behind, reflected in the pool and seen for the first time as they were and are. Then a cloud passes overhead and the pool is empty. The fragile moment is gone before the speaker can lay hold of it to analyze its meaning, and there remains the sound of children laughing and a strange sense of exhilaration. Derek Traversi comments that

> the voice of the bird, recalling the initial 'deception of the thrush', comes back with renewed urgency to expel the dreamers from the 'first world', to assert their normal inability, as time-conditioned creatures living in and limited by 'the present', to hold to what may be, on another, scarcely apprehensible level, 'reality.'[8]

We have at the outset of "Burnt Norton" the remembrance of a moment of intense consciousness, one in which "reality" is perceived, howbeit dimly, and misinterpreted. In the end such experience is not trustworthy. It is not really possible to hold present and future together by delving into the dark recesses of one's personal past. We must acknowledge the overwhelming dominance of time present in which the deepest dilemmas must be resolved, if in fact that is at all possible.

The nature of the experience so briefly and unsatisfactorily perceived in the rose garden is in part two of "Burnt Norton" described in terms of an order that reconciles, and thus unites, opposites. All is in seeming flux, contraries straining against one another, and yet they are unified in the tension. On the surface there is such correspondency in the pattern of existence that we affirm the reconciliation of opposites "among the stars." The essential point of the section beginning "Garlic and sapphires in the mud," through the twin images of boarhound and boar, is to be found in the lines that follow: "At the still point of the turning world" where the dance is—the dance that reflects the ultimate stillness. This stillness is dynamic, not static, holding all in vibrant tension to produce the harmonic sound identified by the ancients as the music of the spheres. Through this tension, this Heraclitean harmony, the unified and unanalyzable whole is perceived—albeit indirectly. The perception is in a sense awesome and even frightening, impinging as it does on our common assumptions and sensibilities. It involves a suspension of the ordinary, of what Eliot calls "practical desire," of suffering and acting, and results in an intuition of an entirely new world of experience in which the old is understood anew and in some way fulfilled.

In the last lines of this section Eliot considers the bondage in time, time past and time future, combined with our present finitude, our bodily weakness, the bondage that is perhaps necessary. After the vision in the rose garden, the vision that faded away as the cloud covered the sun, the poet acknowledged the necessity of its fading with the admission that human beings could not stand very much reality. Now Eliot harks back to that statement with his reflection on heaven and hell ("damnation")— the final either/or to which the soul is destined. Ecstasy and horror become ecstasy *or* horror in the final event. There is no Dantean *limbo*. Thus bondage to time saves us from that reality which in our condition as humans we cannot bear. Only as we

11

submit ourselves to a daily routine of discipline, following the teachings of such spiritual masters as the mystics, can the fleeting, partial, imperfect illumination become not only endurable, but applicable to daily existence. This will be the message of part three of "Burnt Norton." The way up is not at all satisfactory. The poet will have to go on to explore "the way down."

Eliot closes this section with a kind of reprise on the opening theme, a further meditation on time. He confronts a paradox, "To be conscious is not to be in time," and concludes that only in time can the moments of intense consciousness—the rose garden, the rain in the arbor, the draughty church—occur and be remembered. Thus it is that such moments are impermanent and partial. And yet: "Only through time time is conquered."

The third movement of "Burnt Norton" expresses through images the meaning of our temporal enchainment. The images conjure up a dark, depressing scene dominated by common humanity mired in humdrum existence. We find ourselves in the London Underground, where the people we encounter reveal

> Neither plenitude nor vacancy. Only a flicker
> Over the strained time-ridden faces
> Distracted from distraction by distraction. . . .
>
> Men and bits of paper, whirled by the cold wind
> That blows before and after time,
> Wind in and out of unwholesome lungs
> Time before and time after.

The picture presented is reminiscent of the procession of the damned over London Bridge in *The Waste Land*. The impression given by Eliot in this scene, Steffan Bergsten remarks, is wholly negative. "Its only meaning lies in the abasement of life it suggests—so far is the soul removed from the Divine as not even to feel its own deprivation. The spirit, the breath of eternity, is unknown in this modern Limbo where another wind is whirling—the 'cold wind/ That blows before and after time.' It is 'faded air.' "[9] The description of the crowd here looks back to the images of paralysis in *The Hollow Men*. Here are the spiritually blind, characters like Amy and the aunts and uncles of *The Family Reunion* who inhabit a shallow and insensitive and cruel, twittering world.

It is perhaps the meaningless and cruel chatter of such respectable, shallow folk that Eliot has in mind when he speaks of "wind in and out of unwholesome lungs/ Time before and time after...," sweeping over and through London and its millions, over and through the comfortable suburbs. This is a twilight kingdom, wholly self-contained, a "twittering world" in which there is no awareness of darkness, especially not of the darkness through which we grope to attain salvation. Or so it seems. But now we are made suddenly aware that the way up is the way down; the way toward the "still point" of the world is through this twilight kingdom. We must, the poet says, descend as the escalator descends, as the lift descends at the Gloucester Road Underground Station, descend into "the world of perpetual solitude." The challenge now is to accept existence in time and to be submerged in time, going down, going ever lower, as indicated by Heraclitus and as described, with directions, by St. John of the Cross. The way up is the way down, the gradual descent into utter darkness, in three discernible stages: negation or desiccation first of the senses, then of fancy or intellect, and finally of the spirit as well. This is the deliberate descent into darkness whereby the light, the heart of light at the still point where the dance is, may be perceived. Here is the first glimpse in these poems of the mystic way of ascent to beatitude by means of descent into darkness—the negative way.

The descent which is ascent is by way of death and issues in resurrection. So the fourth movement of "Burnt Norton" seems to say, a poem whose shape is reminiscent of a pattern poem, like that of George Herbert's *Easter Wings*. It is seemingly based on another immediate experience of intense consciousness. While visiting the Society of the Sacred Mission at Kelham, Eliot went for a walk and happened upon Avesham Church. There he observed a great yew in the churchyard (symbol of death and immortality), masses of clematis in the rectory garden, and a stream running by on its way to the River Trent. It was a cloudy, perhaps rainy, day. It might have been "the moment in the arbour where the rain beat." At the stream Eliot caught sight of a kingfisher, a bird of brilliant plumage, darting through the air like an arrow. For centuries the kingfisher has been regarded with awe, and Sir Thomas Browne writes, "A kingfisher hung by the bill sheweth where the wind is." The kingfisher was also identified as the halcyon of the ancients and so with halcyon days, the fourteen days of calm about the winter solstice while the bird is nesting, days of stillness. In a moment of intense consciousness Eliot sees the kingfisher dart away and a ray of sunlight piercing the gloom, reflected off the bird's bright wing. Then and there, I would propose, the poet caught a glimpse of reality. That momentary perception broke the gloomy trend of his thoughts in the churchyard, dread thoughts of futility, despair, and death. It is as though he descended into the depths and there caught sight of light, the light at the still point of the turning world, the light that reveals the promise of resurrection and new life.

Such an understanding, whether exactly as put here or not, is confirmed and strengthened by the wing-shape of the poem and by the words, the sounds, and the music. The poem is carefully constructed to say (any paraphrase is less than adequate) that in the twilight of life, our life and the world's existence, when all creation is urged to turn to mankind for light and life, the hopelessness of unwarranted expectation is apparent. Standing in

Avesham churchyard, the poet knows depression and descends into the depths. All around him are symbols of finitude, of the hollowness of human pretensions to omnipotence and omniscience. At that moment he is in a state of humility so intensely felt that he is freed from his innate blindness. He perceives, as the kingfisher darts up, a ray of sunlight reflected on the bird's wing and followed by silence, and he knows that "the light is still/ At the still point of the turning world." Thus Eliot perceives the source of light and life, through the depths, in the darkest night, at the still point which Beatrice in Dante's *Paradiso* hails, saying, "From that one Point are hung the heavens and all nature's law" (28:41-2).

In the end is the contrast between this twilight world which is neither light nor dark, symbolized by the London Underground and the passengers in it, and the darkness through which the ultimate light shines, giving life and hope. Between this twittering, clamorous, restless world and the stillness, "the world of perpetual solitude," from whence issues the dance, meaning and life, there is an immense gulf fixed.

In the lyric we are led down into darkness and then at the turning point move up toward the ultimate light, at the still point of the turning world. As we read the lines it is the poet's intent that we experience the meaning and be so caught up in the pattern, the mood, the music of the poem that we are grasped and influenced, experiencing the quiet, profound joy with which it ends. For that to happen, however, there must be present that quality which permeates the heart of the poem: humility. We must be available and expectant as we read,

> Time and the bell have buried the day,
> The black cloud carries the sun away.
> Will the sunflower turn to us, will the clematis
> Stray down, bend to us. . . ?

> After the kingfisher's wing
> Has answered light to light, and is silent, the light is still
> At the still point of the turning world.

15

In the final movement of "Burnt Norton" Eliot returns to
themes established in the first movement, the problem of words
for the poet and the meaning of the fleeting vision in the rose
garden, which he treats in the second part of this movement. At
the outset the ideal is explained:

> Words, after speech, reach
> Into the silence. Only by the form, the pattern,
> Can words or music reach
> The stillness, as a Chinese jar still
> Moves perpetually in its stillness.

In the quest for the wholeness beyond chaos, timelessness
beyond time, and meaning beyond meaninglessness, Eliot looks
to art, the art of the potter, the painter, the musician, the poet.
The arts are a possible means to wholeness because they do not
seek to analyze, to tear the original and ultimate unity apart into
discreet pieces, but rather through form and pattern seek to
represent the stillness at the still point of the turning world. The
poet uses words, which are parts and pieces of the whole. By
arranging words in patterns the poet can reach beyond the words
themselves to their unified, ultimate meaning. But it is never a
simple process, for "words strain,/ Crack and sometimes break,
under the burden." They will not remain still. It is as if words
try to resist the pattern. If they resist it may be due to forces
lacking in the poet, but it may also be due to hostile forces or
powers attacking, as the "voices of temptation" attacked Christ,
the "Word in the desert."

Here is a key: the Word/Logos/Incarnation, the intersection
of time by timelessness. Thus we reflect back upon the passage
and realize the juxtaposition of words and Word. The same kind
of juxtaposition occurs in *Choruses from "The Rock"* I ("Knowledge of words, and ignorance of the Word"). Here both words
and Word are assailed by the voices of temptation and projected

into self-pity and delusion, perhaps because both words and Word concern the reality at the still point, words reaching for the Word which reaches for words. That this is important to Eliot can be confirmed by looking at the opening lines of *Ash Wednesday* V.

The pattern is now clearer. It is likened to stairs, stairs reminiscent of the ten steps of the ladder of love in St. John of the Cross's *The Dark Night of the Soul.* To descend the stairs from desire to love is to descend in humility, and this is the essential pattern.

> Desire itself is movement
> Not in itself desireable;
> Love is itself unmoving,
> Only the cause and end of movement,
> Timeless and undesiring. . . .

The way towards the whole, and thus towards meaning, is finally perceived in terms of the fulfillment of desire in love, love which is itself the beginning and end of movement, the unmoved Mover of Aristotle's *Metaphysics,* where the Eternal is perceived and desired. The goal of our search is now beginning to assume the characteristics of the personal. For if desire is fulfilled in love, then desire is the dim and partial reflection of its source and end, the One who loves us.

In the final lines of the fifth movement we return to the rose garden, but now with the insight that the movement of intense consciousness experienced there is a revelation of what can exist here, now and always, by pursuit of the way down (which is the way up) and by spiritual discipline, which is the way of humility. We end perhaps with a strong sense of incompleteness, but with hope and some wisdom which will point the way toward reality. What has been learned? One critic puts it well: "Time is redeemed. . . by accepting memory (past) while one moves toward desire (future) controlled by love (the constant now of the present)."[10] This insight will be tested time and again in the rest of the poem; it will not be altered, at least not critically.

17

iii. EAST COKER

"Burnt Norton" was published in 1935; its sequel, "East Coker," appeared first as a supplement to the *New English Weekly* in March of 1940. The writing, publication, and first reading of the poem took place in the context of World War II. "East Coker" was written in wartime and was read by people experiencing the boredom and the terrors of war. In September of that year a fourth printing of the supplement appeared. On September 7 the first major air raids on London occurred. Mollie Panter-Downes, reporting on the beginnings of the Battle of Britain, wrote on September 14:

> For Londoners, there are no longer such things as good nights; there are only bad nights, worse nights, and better nights. The sirens go off at approximately the same time every evening, and in the poorer districts, queues of people carrying blankets, thermos flasks, and babies begin to form quite early outside the air-raid shelters. The *Blitzkrieg* continues to be directed against such military objectives as the tired shopgirl, the red-eyed clerk, and the thousands of dazed and weary families patiently trundling their few belongings in perambulators away from the wreckage of their homes.[11]

The omnipresent fact of war must be kept in mind here and for the rest of the sequence of poems.

"East Coker" begins not with an overt reference to the war but rather with remembrance of another particular experience: the poet's journey to the place of his ancestors, East Coker in Somerset, not far from Yeovil. The opening statement, by way of prelude, "In my beginning is my end," is an inversion of Mary

19

Queen of Scots' motto, "En ma fin est mon commencement," and provides a key to the meaning of "East Coker." The poet seems to say that through examination of his distant familial beginnings he can find the purpose of his life. "Burnt Norton" treated this theme, too, but in a different way, since it is preoccupied with the vision in the rose garden and its alternative, the disciplining of the soul by means of ascetic exercises, called "the way down." Here the statement "In my beginning is my end" suggests not so much the endless circularity of change and decay as that which gives meaning to this circularity. Here "end" means not so much termination as purpose, and "beginning" a movement out of time into a world without time. The critic David Ward says, "This 'beginning' is the purpose, or end, of a life, as it is also the ending of an old life. And, thus, too, beginning in the sense of being born implies not only the end in death, but the purpose of assuming new life."[12]

With this thought in mind, the poet remembers a time when he descended by a narrow road into the village of East Coker and to a field noted for its prehistoric dancing circle. It was a warm, hazy summer day. There in the field he looked beyond the relatively recent Eliot past to an old, old order in the far distant past, and invokes a village wedding dance in the open field, on a "summer midnight":

> A dignified and commodious sacrament.
> Two and two, necessarye coniunction,
> Holding eche other by the hand or the arm
> Which betokeneth concorde.

Eliot is citing the sixteenth-century Sir Thomas Elyot's *A Book Named the Governor* (1.21). In that book men and women are presented as opposites, contraries united, harmonized in the religiously significant ritual dance. As such the dance reflects symbolically the harmony of the spheres, the order which the Tudor Elyot contrasted to the surrounding, ever threatening chaos. In the pagan ritual of the summer solstice at the dancing circle, the very essence of the natural order was revealed in its characteristic fertility, its society, and its concord. The dance is of the earth, earthy, and yet its source is the unified whole which it represents.

The dance also signifies the ritual of matrimony, the coming together of individuals in obedience to the social imperative of procreation, the creation of new life in the context of mortality, without which society ceases to exist. In procreation men and women participate in the necessary rhythm of the natural order, and thus participate in harmony and concord. Richard Hooker in Book 5 of his *Lawes* expressed the same fundamentally earthy, significant point of view: "In this world there can be no societie durable otherwise then onlie by propagation. Albeit therefore single life be a thing more angelicall and divine, yeat sith the replenishing first of earth with blessed inhabitantes and then of heaven with Sainctes everlastinglie praysing God did depend upon conjunction of man and woman, he which made all thinges complete and perfect saw it could not be good to leave man without an helper. . . ." (73.1) And the 1559 *Book of Common Prayer* made the same point, but added that matrimony is also "for the mutual society, help, and comfort" of men and women conjoined in wedlock to propagate and to avoid sin.

At the end of the first movement of "East Coker" the night is past and the vision of the dancing circle is over. The poet faces a new day. In the light of day he concludes that the past is not for him; the rhythms and rituals of the distant past are not recoverable, for they have not been transmitted. All is flux and uncertainty. Each moment we must begin again at the beginning. From another perspective we might say that the poet has discovered that the meaning of the still point is not to be found in partial visions or partial horrors. The meaning is not to be found in contemplation of strange, past events. The meaning is here, now, wherever we are in the time frame in which we exist. This is affirmation.

Having turned away from East Coker, away from the place where his ancestors lie buried, away from the dancing circle and all that it seemed to imply in his vision of the far distant past, the poet is ready to leave the past behind and to begin again in the present. Such affirmation is rightly understood in the context of

Eliot's life and of the time—the time of false war and then of *blitzkrieg,* when many first read "East Coker"—when doubts were rampant, chaos threatening to engulf rationality, the spectre of death haunting everyone nightly, and faith in reality fragile at best.

In the second movement, by contrast to his perception of ancient order at East Coker and by contrast to the vision of order presented in the second movement of "Burnt Norton," Eliot points to the present chaos. All order is gone. The disorder, chaos, and flux characteristic of Europe in 1940 dominate his thoughts. The end of the world is heralded by the shattering of the once steadfast rhythms of nature, of earth, and of the cosmic cycles. As you read, listen to the lyric, the music, the archaic tetrameters controlling the explosive observations:

> What is late November doing
> With the disturbance of the spring
> And creatures of the summer heat. . . ?
>
> Thunder rolled by the rolling stars
> Simulates triumphal cars. . .
>
> Whirled in a vortex that shall bring
> The world to that destructive fire
> Which burns before the ice-cap reigns.

Eliot proceeds to express his dismay of ever finding that order, bringing meaning and wholeness, for which he seeks; the order familiar, if not dominant, to the lives of the ancients at East Coker. Furthermore he recognizes that the "elders" are now unable to assist him in his quest, and questions the value of old age's dignity and wisdom:

> Had they deceived us
> Or deceived themselves, the quiet-voiced elders,
> Bequeathing us merely a receipt for deceit?

The poet is shaken, uncertain, and beseiged by doubts. His condition is understandable. What we learn from the past is second-hand at best. It has been scrutinized and analyzed and is thus distorted, even falsified.

> The knowledge imposes a pattern, and falsifies
> For the pattern is new in every moment
> And every moment is a new and shocking
> Valuation of all we have been.

Eliot is here dealing with a perennial problem. Reality is to be received and not imposed; it is to be received from another and not from ourselves. Yet in the process of receiving it we are inclined to impose our own meaning on reality, and thus we destroy it. This is sin. The opposite of sin is the humble reception of that which is offered, however discomforting it may be— denouncing our selfish inclinations, denying us our cherished pleasures, and shocking us out of complacency into reality. To be shocked thus is to live.[13] The pattern imposed is untrue, an illusion, death. The pattern received is revelation, renewing its recipients.

What is needed, if the pattern is to be received and we are to avoid the chaos and experience the eternal order as the ancients knew it, is humility. And so the poet writes,

> O do not let me hear
> Of the wisdom of old men, but rather of their folly. . .

> The only wisdom we can hope to acquire
> Is the wisdom of humility; humility is endless.

We have arrived at another turning point in this sequence of poems. For the first time Eliot speaks of God as God. Various other names or symbols have been used to denote God heretofore, but now the poet, a devout Anglican who converted in 1927 before this sequence of poems was begun, a faithful communicant, regular in making his confession, begins to speak in words that overtly and definitely indicate his faith and his Christian practice, as well as his trust in the pattern as given in and through the Church. And yet Eliot still exercises reserve; he prefers by and large to avoid the specialized language of traditional Christian theology.

For the time being we must be content to observe that Eliot gives humility priority in relation to other sacred virtues, as did Bernard of Clairvaux who, commenting on Benedict of Nursia's *Regula*, interpreted "I am the way, the truth, the life" in John's gospel as "Humility (is) the way that leads to truth," while truth is "the light of life." In his sermon on *The Nature of Pride*, Richard Hooker spoke of humility as the basis of "the peace of the world." Lancelot Andrewes tells us that humility is rooted and grounded in the humility of Christ, who was humble even to the point of death on the Cross. This humility is what the Roman Catholic existentialist, Gabriel Marcel, spoke of as "availability." Availability is that which makes ready and makes room for otherness. It is openness to what is outside and beyond, and it is receptivity to the existence and power of another, of others, and of the Other. It is that which Marcel means when he writes, "The spirit of prayer is, above all, a welcoming disposition towards everything which can tear me away from myself, from my propensity to become hypnotised by my own faults."[14] Such, too, is the kind of humility to which Eliot refers.

The third movement of "East Coker" begins with a passage that echoes Samson's opening speech in Milton's *Samson Agonistes*. It describes the darkness at the noon of the day, the extinction of civilization: "O dark, dark, dark. They all go into the dark,/ The vacant intersellar spaces, the vacant into the vacant. . . ." The way lies through the present darkness, the darkness which is the darkness of God, there in darkness to await illumination. This way of putting it provides another way of defining humility.

Eliot uses the image of the London subway again, but now there is no purposeful descent. Now there is only the aimless movement of bodies in time and space. It would seem that the poet is summoning the human soul to awareness of its actual situation by confronting the illusory nature of so-called reality (the theatre scenery), the vacancy or emptiness behind seeming vitality (the Underground passengers), and the horrible paradox of being conscious—but conscious of nothing (the patient under ether). This encounter with the actual is painful but necessary, involving abandonment of fond illusions and a growing openness to and awareness of reality, the reality of the still point represented in time by the pattern, the dance. Eliot is, of course, referring to abandonment of illusions and falsities, to await revelation in humility.

This is the *via negativa* described by St. John of the Cross. It involves renunciation of hope and love, for hope and love would be for the wrong things, that is, for things of our own choosing, concerning patterns we would create and then seek to impose upon the chaos around us. We must learn to wait, humbly and in faith; "the faith and the love and the hope" are not in the doing, not in desperate, futile activity. They are to be found through waiting.

The third movement of "East Coker" comes to a close with a classic restatement of the *via negativa* found in St. John of the Cross's *Ascent of Mt. Carmel*:

> In order to arrive at having pleasure in everything,
> Desire to have pleasure is nothing.
> In order to arrive at possessing everything,
> Desire to possess nothing.
> In order to arrive at knowing everything,
> Desire to know nothing. . . . (1.13)

Eliot's lines are one way of expressing Christian humility, the humbling of Christ upon the Cross, the sacrificial love revealed to those who respond with humility and sacrificial love. The lines are a dramatic expression of the dictum in Christ's saying, "He who finds his life will lose it, and he who loses his life for my sake will find it" (Mt. 10:39).

The lyric fourth movement that follows presents the pattern, the pattern as transmitted by the Christian gospel. The pattern is atonement, a dynamic and not static occurrence, restoring the lost order, unity, and wholeness of eternity. The poem is similar to some verses of the metaphysical poets of the seventeenth century, involving an elaborate conceit, and it is partially influenced by Sir Thomas Browne's *Religio Medici*, where we read: "For the world, I count not an Inn, but an Hospital, and a place, not to live in, but to die in." And it constitutes another key turning point, for now to the metaphysic of "Burnt Norton" there is added the gospel in such a way that there can be no doubt that the metaphysic is fulfilled, overshadowed, and transformed. In a letter, Eliot had referred to part four of "East Coker" as "the heart of the matter."[15] In a sense the lyric is a Good Friday meditation on the Lord, who by the Incarnation accepts a personal death and becomes the wounded one as well as the one who comes to heal. The poem proceeds here as a series of paradoxes:

The wounded surgeon plies the steel. . . .

Our only health is the disease
If we obey the dying nurse. . . .

The whole earth is our hospital
Endowed by the ruined millionaire,

26

Wherein, if we do well, we shall
Die of the absolute paternal care. . . .

If to be warmed, then I must freeze
And quake in frigid purgatorial fires
Of which the flame is roses, and the smoke is briars. . . .

Again, in spite of that, we call this Friday good.

Eliot here presents the gospel by way of an analogy carefully
devised to avoid over-used and unnecessary biblical and theological
terms. Simply stated, humanity is chronically ill. The disease is
sin. Sin, however defined, and Eliot defines it in various ways, is
principally that self-centeredness that prevents our ability to
receive the gospel. Because this sin is also the means by which we
are cured, it must grow worse before it can be recognized for what
it is and be excised. The cure is effected by the Lord, the
wounded surgeon, who is full of compassion, who operates
through the dying nurse, the Church.

Eliot is careful to point out that the Church is not here to
please us, but to remind us of our sin. A vital part of our cure,
that which makes us accessible to the ministrations of the
wounded surgeon, is recognition of our sin, recognition that leads
to contrition and repentance. But most important is the love that
the Creator has for us, providing "the absolute paternal care,"
love manifested through chastisement and discipline, but most of
all through his self-offering, his giving of his own in the Incarnate
Lord offered upon the altar of the Cross and on the altar of the
Eucharist. It is in the context of the Eucharist that the saving,
painful, yet glorious ministration of the divine surgeon normally
occurs. Here in the sacrament we "spiritually eat the flesh of
Christ and drink his blood"; we are in Christ as Christ is in us; we
who are many are one in Christ as Christ is in us all. Our dying
life is wedded to the Christ who died and dies daily with and for
us. Christ's risen life and his healing sacramental power are active
in our hospital world, our dying society.

A further thought is offered by Derek Traversi:

By a final paradox, we are enabled to see as 'good' the Friday which consummated the apparently final death and defeat of Christ—and, through our association with the atoning action, of ourselves—by the forces of evil and death. The paradox indeed, with its intimation of life as springing from death, presents itself as a central turning-point for the entire sequence.[16]

The fourth verse of this section is of particular interest in relation to the lyric fourth movement of "Burnt Norton." The connection is established by means of the word *chill*, the word that stands at the center of the earliest lyric. Here in the present poem the chill—chill death—creeps up our legs, threatening to engulf us. The fever that attends the chill influences our mental processes. Paradoxically, to possess the warmth of life we must necessarily be "chilled," freeze in purgatorial fires, whereby the imperfection of our desire is cleansed by Love, the wounded surgeon. Various influences seem to be operating on the poet at this point: Dante's characterization of the medieval poet, Arnaut Daniel, in the *Purgatorio*, and the metaphysical poets in particular. Henry Vaughan's poem "Love-sick" comes to mind, especially these lines:

> O come and rend,
> Or bow the heavens! Lord bow them and descend,
> And at thy presence make these mountains flow,
> These mountains of cold Ice in me! Thou art
> Refining fire, O then refine my heart,
> My foul, foul heart! Thou art immortall heat,
> Heat motion gives; Then warm it, till it beat,
> So beat for thee, till thou in mercy hear. . . .

Out of the flames of the purgatorial fire come roses, roses as flames symbolizing eternal life, and their smoke is briars, briars that both wound and redeem. We must remember that the roses of the rose garden in "Burnt Norton" represent desire. The roses flaming out of the purgatorial fire are those roses transformed to represent the fulfillment of desire in Love and thus eternal life. The latter image of roses does not negate the

28

former: desire is where we begin in time and space on our journey toward fulfillment in Love.

In the light of the pattern perceived in the Christian gospel, the poet's skills are judged and found wanting at the outset of the fifth movement of "East Coker." As soon as the reality is received, it is analyzed, distorted, and falsified. The poem is, then, a failure. And yet the poet must keep on trying.

> There is only the fight to recover what has been lost
> And found and lost again and again. . . .

> For us, there is only the trying. The rest is not our business.

In the end the poet muses that home is not the place of our ancestors, as he had thought it might be on his journey to East Coker, nor of our childhood, the seeming focus of "Burnt Norton." Rather it is the present, the immediate moment of each new beginning. Our quest is not realizable in the past or in the future. If it is to be carried out at all, it must be done in the present. One reason why this is so has to do with the nature of the quest for ultimate reality as involving immediate experience. It is the quest for love coming from beyond all space and time, love toward which desire yearns love which is to be known now or not at all, in that which becomes and is the eternal now. Therefore,

> Old men ought to be explorers
> Here and there does not matter
> We must keep still and still moving
> Into another intensity
> For a further union, a deeper communion
> Through the dark cold and the empty desolation. . . .

That is to say, old men must be still in awaiting the revelation—
not imposing some pattern of their own devising upon the present.
They must be "still moving," prepared to accept what is, living,
striving, laboring in the present for the realization and fulfillment
of desire in love. They must keep on working in the present
through which alone time is redeemed, avoiding the temptation
to live in the past or to give themselves over to some illusory
solution, some refuge which prevents them from meeting challenges. And they must grapple with these challenges in the light
of as much of revelation as they perceive, thus moving onward
into a deeper, more intense communion—love. What is required is
humility, supported by conviction and dedication. The end or
purpose is to keep on receiving and thus to keep on journeying
toward "a further union, a deeper communion." The closing lines
point forward to "The Dry Salvages" and the final "In my end is
my beginning"—the Queen of Scots' motto given as she gave
it—points towards the goal of deeper communion and to that
death which issues in eternal life.

*****

It is illuminating to consider East Coker with Dante's four
levels of meaning in mind. On the literal level it would seem that
this quartet has to do with the journey of the poet, conscious of
his advancing age, into his past, which is the distant past of his
race and of his species. Indeed, it is a journey to that earth where
the past lays buried. On the moral level, the poem concerns
humility, although Gardner is right in saying that in doing this
"East Coker" accepts "the necessity of humility in *Burnt Norton*.
. . . But it adds to the acceptance of ignorance in *Burnt Norton* an
act of faith. It declares that the darkness is the darkness of God
and waits upon him."[17] On the mystical level the poem concerns
the *via negativa*, which is alluded to most prominently in the third

movement. On the allegorical level proper, the poem concerns Atonement, the action of Christ for our salvation in the death on the Cross and the sacrifice of the Eucharist.

iv. THE DRY SALVAGES

"The Dry Salvages," named for a group of rocks (presumably *les trois sauvages*) off Cape Ann in Massachusetts where Eliot spent his summers as a child, was written at a time when he was preoccupied with the Battle of Britain. Written in January of 1941, the quartet was published in *The New English Weekly* on 27 February. This was a time when Britain suffered great losses and was locked into its island fortress. There was some hope, a counter-offensive against the Italian army in North Africa having begun the previous December and the Libyan port of Benghazi falling at the beginning of February. There was a lull in the air battle over London, but other cities were being pounded by the Nazis. The center of Coventry Cathedral was destroyed the previous November, the New Year was greeted in London with fire raids, and incendiaries destroyed Wren churches such as St. Lawrence Jewry and St. Andrew-by-the-Wardrobe, the fires consuming slums and palaces alike with great loss of life. There was a mood of waiting in London. Mollie Panter-Downes reports on February 9:

> Both informed and uninformed opinion seems to be that the curtain may go up at any moment. Every few days, the press discovers some new and absolutely infallible date for the attempt to invade Britain. . . . Most people seem to think that though Hitler may not obligingly fit his actions in with the journalists' predictions, something will certainly be tried soon—a frame of mind which makes all small personal planning for the future seem futile. . . .[18]

In the beginning months of 1941 Eliot's thoughts must often have turned toward his American homeland, to the convoys providing a lifeline over the Atlantic, to the sailors striving heroically and dying bravely for the sake of a dying civilization.

In the first movement of the poem Eliot writes of the river and the sea, the Mississippi River which was his dread companion as he grew up in St. Louis, and the Atlantic Ocean by whose shores his family spent summers and Tom sailed, sometimes around the Dry Salvages, the silent but significant rocks looming above water at low tide and still there, submerged and dangerous, at high tide. The river and the sea also suggest to him the dark forces threatening human complacency, human confidence in ingenuity and indifference to the unknown. For Eliot, the river within and the sea without are both ominous.

Eliot remembers something unspecified and deeply disturbing there, by the river, "in the rank ailanthus of the April dooryard,/ In the smell of grapes on the autumn table. . . ." What he remembers may be an omnipresent dark force threatening destruction, a force we try to ignore and sometimes succeed in forgetting, but cannot thereby vanquish. The sea, like the river, is disturbing, threatening the very ground of existence. In later life Eliot perceived both river and sea as symbols not only of present threats but of past agonies. We can only guess at what they might be, concretely and actually, but in some sense they reminded the poet of all that contributed to his sense of *angst*, his doubt concerning purpose in life and in his life in particular.

Then over the sea sounds there tolls a bell, rung by the ground swell of the sea—the 'ground of being,' if you will allow a phrase that Eliot would most likely not use.

> The tolling bell
> Measures time not our time, rung by the unhurried
> Ground swell, a time
> Older than the time of chronometers. . . .

The poet hears the bell tolling and, while listening, experiences a moment of apprehension which is also a moment of revelation—an annunciation. The bell rings, reminding him of his death, but

this is not the passing bell of John Donne's *Devotions*. This is the
bell rung "by the unhurried/ Ground swell," measuring time. It
is not our time, not chronological time, but time stemming from
eternity. This is not the time of those women waiting at
Gloucester harbor and every such harbor for fishermen to return
from the sea, waiting with growing anxiety and lying awake
wondering "What if?" and "What then?" The past is deceptive
and "future futureless." At the end of this movement the bell
tolls, rung not by humans but by nature, by that which is now
and always, by eternity. A moment of apprehension becomes a
moment of annunciation as the bell rings reminding us now not
only of death but also of new life, rebirth, eternal life. The image
of the bell is being transformed; later in this poem it becomes the
bell at the Angelus. For those women who wait it is the morning
watch but when we listen in the pre-dawn darkness, hearing the
bell ring, rung by no human power, we sense the intersection of
time and timelessness and are summoned out of anxiety to prayer.

Helen Gardner, commenting on the last three lines of this
section, suggests they are reminiscent of the doxology, and thus
give us

> the implication of the symbol of the ground swell, which
> makes itself felt in our hearts by the bell. The bell sounds a
> warning and a summons: it demands a response. Like the
> Angelus it is a call to prayer, and a commemoration of the
> mystery of the Incarnation; like the bell at the consecration
> it is a call to worship, and announces the presence of Christ;
> like the tolling bell it reminds us of our death, and calls us to
> die daily.[19]

The symbolism here is very rich, and operates on a number of
levels.

The lyric that begins the second movement of "The Dry

Salvages" expresses despair that enchainment in time, the ceaseless threat of river and sea and all past agonies, will never end. It expresses the fear that there is in fact no end, no purpose, that all is ultimately suffused in horror and meaninglessness. The mood is that of Gerard Manley Hopkins' poem, "The Leaden Echo": "Be beginning to despair, to despair,/ Despair, despair, despair, despair." As in Hopkins' poem the last word belongs to its sequel, "The Golden Echo," so here there is ground for hope beyond despair. There is an end, death, which contains the promise of birth and thus leads the poet to remember 'the one Annunciation' —the prayer of Mary involving death to self and surrender to God's will, which is true humility and leads to the promise of new birth in eternal life. So Eliot writes,

> There is no end of it, the voiceless wailing,
> No end . . .
> To the drift of the sea and the drifting wreckage,
> The bone's prayer to Death its God. Only the hardly,
> > barely prayable
> Prayer of the one Annunciation.

In the lyric of the second movement of "Burnt Norton," Eliot testified to the reconciliation of opposites "among the stars"—the eternal order. In "East Coker," at the equivalent place, he testified to the breakdown of that order in flux and chaos. Now he claims that the only end to that disorder is in the response of self-surrender to the eternal manifest in time. W.H. Auden expressed that response in his poem "The Annunciation," where Mary's speech is full of awe and joy: "My flesh in terror and fire/ Rejoices that the Word . . ./ Should ask to wear me/ From now to their wedding day,/ For an engagement ring." In another poem, also called "The Annunciation," Edwin Muir emphasized the encounter between Mary and the angel, and its strangeness:

> He's come to her
> From far beyond the farthest star,
> Feathered through time. Immediacy

36

Of strangest strangeness is the bliss
That from their limbs all movement takes.
Yet the increasing rapture brings
So great a wonder that it makes
Each feather tremble on his wings.

John V. Taylor in his book *The Go-Between God* links Mary's
experience to all annunciations, the "one Annunciation" being
the archetype for all the rest. The Annunciation is marked by the
intense consciousness of the unanalyzable whole, now perceived
to be the God who sends the Incarnate One, the wounded surgeon,
to our rescue. It is possible because God is in fact love, and Mary
is humbly receptive. The Annunciation thus involves the meeting
of I and Thou, a "current of communication," the "invisible go-
between" whom Christians call the Holy Spirit, the Spirit of God.
This is "the Spirit which possessed and dominated the man Jesus
Christ, making him the most aware and sensitive and open human
being who has ever lived—ceaselessly aware of God. . . ."[20] And so
in a sense, given such an understanding of this lyric beginning of
the second movement of "Dry Salvages," the lyric opening of
"Burnt Norton" 2 represents the ideal that was and that shall be,
and the lyric opening of "East Coker" 2 represents the actual
situation in the nineteen-forties. The lyric opening of "The Dry
Salvages" 2 represents the ground of hope for us in the one
Annunciation, and in such annunciations as flow from it and are
in some way representative of it.

 After the lyric movement, the poet reflects upon his realization that the revelation received through the intersection of time
by the timeless restores past experiences with new and vital
meaning that exceeds anything he has hitherto imagined. In
moments of illumination there is a heightened sense of awareness
that brings flashes of glory, the perception of truth and beauty,
and also something frightening, unsettling, and disruptive. Such
awareness Eliot describes as

Something that is probably quite ineffable:
The backward look behind the assurance

Of recorded history, the backward half-look
Over the shoulder, towards the primitive terror.

Audrey Cahill comments on these lines,

> The primitive terror without and the primitive terror within
> are also permanent parts of reality, as the women of Canter-
> bury discover in *Murder in the Cathedral*:
>
> > I have consented, Lord Archbishop, have consented.
> > Am torn away, subdued, violated,
> > United to the spiritual flesh of nature,
> > Mastered by the animal powers of spirit,
> > Dominated by the lust of self-demolition.
>
> The 'moments of agony' arise out of the duality of this aware-
> ness: human beings belong to both these spiritual worlds, and
> it is the conflict between them that causes the agony.[21]

Eliot's moments of intense consciousness are now to be understood in the light of the one Annunciation, and in the knowledge
that this experience has been known to others and has been
shared. The agony proceeding from our existence between two
worlds is a shared agony, best understood in relation to the
agonies of others and, supremely, in relation to the agony of
Christ. Knowing this, we know also that

> People change, and smile: but the agony abides.
> Time the destroyer is time the preserver,
> Like the river with its cargo of dead Negroes, cows
>   and chicken coops,
> The bitter apple and the bite in the apple.
> And the ragged rock in the restless waters. . . .

The agony abides; it is only really dangerous when, like the
"ragged rock," it is concealed, suppressed, or otherwise evaded.
Revealed for what it is, it can be transformed and is transformed

by the love that is the Incarnation, time invaded and transformed by the timeless.

The third movement of each of the *Four Quartets* is ordinarily an expansion of what has gone before, and in all of them there is presented the possibility of spiritual progress through detachment. The first three *Quartets* involve significant images of travel, where spiritual progress is discussed in terms of such images. In "Burnt Norton" 3 the flow of time is compared to a train moving "in appetency, on its metalled ways/ Of time past and time future." In "East Coker" 3 the spiritual descent into darkness is compared to a descent underground, descent to a train which stops too long between stations. In "The Dry Salvages" 3 we encounter travellers by train or ocean liner who, in progressing through time, are becoming different people: "You are not those who saw the harbour/ Receding, or those who will disembark."

The heart of the matter in "The Dry Salvages" 3 is a theme which has earlier preoccupied Eliot. To follow in the way of the one Annunciation "into another intensity/ For a further union, a deeper communion" requires self-denial, detachment such as that of which Sri Krishna spoke in the *Gita*, and such as we find expressed in Matthew 6:25-34, "Therefore I tell you, do not be anxious about your life, what you shall eat or what you shall drink. . . ." To live without regard to past or future—to live entirely in the present—requires radical humility, surrender to God's will here and now as each task and challenge is encountered in everyday life. To practice such radical humility is to fare forward on the essential journey, the quest the poet has been pursuing from the beginning of "Burnt Norton." Eliot puts it this way:

> . . . 'on whatever sphere of being
> The mind of a man may be intent
> At the time of death'—that is the one action

(And the time of death is every moment)
Which shall fructify in the lives of others. . . .

The *Bhagavad Gita*, or Song of the Lord, that portion of the great
Indian epic, the *Mahabharata*, says: "When a man frees himself
from attachment to the fruits of Action; Action Itself; or the
objects of the sense world—then hath he reached the highest stage
of right action." Such detachment focuses attention on the quality of our actions, not on their results, and thus finds its fulfillment in the self-surrender of the prayer of the one Annunciation,
"Be it unto me according to thy word." That prayer is not at all
concerned for results or fruits or any such thing, but is totally
involved in the I-Thou encounter with the Other. As we see in
Muir's "Annunciation" poem, the response to the Other consists
in action that is total encounter: "through the endless afternoon/
These neither speak nor movement make,/ But stare into their
deepening trance/ As if their gaze would never break." This is not
to say that the results, the fruits, were any less than altogether
momentous, but momentous not because they were sought after
but because they were, instead, received as a consequence of the
encounter.

When we think of the journey, as Cahill remarks, "whether the
voyagers 'come to port' or whether they 'suffer the trial and judge-
ment' of the sea, *this*, the quality of their detachment, is their real
destination. It is towards this state that they must fare forward."[22]

The fourth movement of "Burnt Norton" consisted of the
lyric which spoke of death and resurrection. "East Coker" 4 presented the essential pattern, bridging the gulf between death and
resurrection—the Atonement. Here, the lyric is a prayer to the
Virgin of the one Annunciation. It is a prayer for voyagers and
those they leave behind, for those who lie dead in the sea, and

40

a prayer to one who is at the point where land and sea, time and eternity, meet. It is a prayer for those journeying through life, threatened by the river within and the sea without. It is a prayer that the bell, the Angelus bell, the bell sounded at the most solemn moment of the Eucharist, may be heard and that hearts and minds be opened to receive the proferred gift of love through the illuminating power of the Holy Spirit, the Spirit of God. Love is the pattern and the meaning.

> Lady, whose shrine stands on the promontory,
> Pray for all those who are in ships. . . .

The poet invokes the Virgin's protection on those who make their living at sea and those who mourn the ones who do not return. He calls her

> Figlia del tuo figlio,
> Queen of Heaven. . . .

The prayer is uttered, too, on behalf of those who ended their voyage in the sea

> Or in the dark throat which will not reject them
> Or wherever cannot reach them the sound of the sea bell's
> Perpetual angelus.

The prayer, which has the sound of the bell in its rhythm, focuses of course on Mary, whose life marks the point in history at which eternity entered into time. The line "Figlia del tuo figlio" is translated "Daughter of thy Son," and taken from St. Bernard's prayer in Canto 33 of Dante's *Paradiso*, which begins:

> Virgin Mother, daughter of thy son;
>> humble beyond all creatures and more exalted;
>> predestined turning point of God's intention;
> Thy merit so ennobled human nature
>> that its divine Creator did not scorn
>> to make Himself the creature of His creature.

41

Mary is adored because she is the meeting place of eternity and time, and is nonetheless humble in the face of this astounding fact. Thus the real focus in the poem, while Mary is certainly part of it, falls on the Incarnate One. In the ritual of the Angelus, the prayer which is the collect for the Annunciation in the *Book of Common Prayer* makes this focus clear: "We beseech thee, O Lord, pour thy grace into our hearts, that we who have known the incarnation of thy Son Jesus Christ, announced by an angel to the Virgin Mary, may by his cross and passion be brought unto the glory of his resurrection. . . ." The Annunciation thus can be seen to represent the entire gospel of Jesus Christ. Our only appropriate response to the receiving of the grace for which we pray, grace that comes to us preeminently through the Eucharist, is to surrender humbly, give thanks, and attempt to do God's will for the rest of our days, not concerned for the fruits of action but ever receiving grace and giving thanks in words and deeds of love. To do this is to participate in Christ, which is to participate in the unified and perfect whole, that which is ultimately meaningful and provides meaning to all else. Through this encounter the unanalyzable whole is revealed to be perfect love.

In the final movement of "The Dry Salvages" Eliot asserts that over against false perceptions of reality, against all illusions, there stands that perception of reality at the intersection of time and the timeless, at the still point of the turning world. To apprehend the still point, where the dance is, is an occupation for the saint—

> No occupation either, but something given
> And taken, in a lifetime's death in love,
> Ardour and selflessness and self-surrender.

For most of us there are only hints and guesses, glimpses of that which is called the Incarnation. The Incarnation we now understand as the preeminent symbol of God's revelation in Christ, incorporating all else and extending from the Annunciation to the death, resurrection, and ascension of the Incarnate One, extending as far as the coming of the Holy Spirit at Pentecost. It also suggests that the incarnation of the divine in other modes is comprehensible, and perhaps only comprehensible, in terms of the one Incarnation.

Our perceptions of reality are only

> Hints followed by guesses; and the rest
> Is prayer, observance, discipline, thought and action.

The holy routine of the Church, the Church that constantly witnesses to the reality known to us only fleetingly in moments of intense consciousness that quickly fade, is the trustworthy alternative to the excitement of fragile annunciations. Since it is trustworthy, the routine may indeed be preferred by those who lack the ardour of spiritual athletes.

The point here must not be passed over lightly, for it deserves serious attention. Eliot has, as usual, carefully worded what he has to say, indicating that in and through the holy routine of the Church we are in vital contact with reality whether we be intensely conscious of it at every moment or not. Note how the poet arranges the sequence of "prayer, observance, discipline, thought and action." Prayer consists of holy desires reaching for eternal love; it is expressed by individuals living in communities of those who profess to be in Christ. Prayer is, in George Herbert's poem of that title,

> Church-bels beyond the starres heard, the souls bloud,
> The land of spices; something understood.

Observance is the disciplined, regular observance of the church year, of feasts and fasts, in the context of the Eucharist, prompting meditation upon and response to the life, passion, and ultimate self-giving of Christ and of the myriad saints following in his way. The spectacular divine drama comes to us in our observance as

43

prayerful and thus humble, yearning worshippers. Discipline, focusing on the sacrament of reconciliation, follows, for it is necessary as we seek to respond to the gift of divine love and surrender as Mary surrendered to God's will. This discipline involves repentance, *metanoia*, turning from self to Other and thus entering into the saving relationship. Such discipline is heralded by Richard Hooker as a potent means of union with God, the fulfillment of our most sincere desire.

The end, product, and fruit of the intersection of time and eternity in prayer, observance, and discipline is to be found in "thought and action." Such thought and action do not involve selfish, willful doing, but rather the cessation of such doing in order that God may act through us. To use Lancelot Andrewes' image, the Christian becomes the willing conduit of divine grace in the world. Thus the Christian life is formed by a pattern composed of prayer, observance, discipline, thought, and action, not performed once for all time but repeated over and over again, in a holy routine that fines and refines the life of the worshipper and, through many worshippers, the life of the community of faith in each particular place.

Once more, however, the poet cautions that for most of us union with God, involving the ability always to perform right actions, is but fragmentarily and incompletely realized. Such perfection is to be found in the incarnate Son and only in him. And so Eliot ends "The Dry Salvages" with a vision of the Atonement. Our goal and purpose, the poet says, can never be realized here; and yet our efforts have value and significance:

> We, content at the last
> If our temporal reversion nourish
> (Not too far from the yew-tree)
> The life of significant soil.

Death is now transformed by love—by the holy routine, the saving pattern, the ultimate order. In "Burnt Norton" there is dread in the words, "Chill/ Fingers of yew be curled/ Down on us." Here, at the end of "The Dry Salvages" there is an echo of the phrase in

"East Coker," "Mirth of those long since under earth/ Nourishing the corn." The trying, however ineffective and faltering it may seem to be, is not futile. It contributes to the nurturing of the dying civilization and is likened to the surrender of the saint and the sacrifice of the martyr. Eliot's image here, "the life of significant soil," echoes those lines in *Murder in the Cathedral* about the sanctity of holy ground, hallowed by a martyr's blood and source of the earth's renewal.[23]

In the literal sense, "The Dry Salvages" concerns experience—the poet's past, our past, the past of our civilization and our race. In the moral sense, it concerns hope, present hope, not hope that the future shall be different from the past, but rather the hope that springs out of our faith and issues in love. In the mystic sense, the sense concerning things spiritual without being confined to any one particular religious experience, "The Dry Salvages" concerns the necessity of cultivating disinterestedness and detachment. We must not look for the fruits of action. We must, rather, live as if there were no future, as if every moment were the moment of death. In the allegorical sense, "The Dry Salvages" concerns annunciation and incarnation. By means of the one Annunciation heralding the Incarnation and by means of the Incarnation which is heralded, time is redeemed, time is intersected by the timeless, and all of our annunciations are made meaningful.

v. LITTLE GIDDING

The last of the *Quartets,* "Little Gidding," was first published in the *New English Weekly* of October 15, 1942, but Eliot possessed a first, rough draft by June 1941, just four months after the publication of "The Dry Salvages." Thus the wartime background of "Little Gidding" was essentially the same as that of the earlier poem. A devastated London, its nights illuminated by the fires of burning buildings and its people struggling to survive amidst harsh living conditions, provides the background for the poet's writing.

In this poem Eliot acknowledges his physical exhaustion and his consciousness of advancing age, accompanied by inevitable physical decay. He was coping with the pain from teeth extractions and learning to live with dentures at the time. He was then concerned not so much with the "hints and guesses" of the previous *Quartets,* the quest for immediate experience of the unified and unanalyzable whole, as with "prayer, observance, discipline, thought and action." The change is obvious in the "immediate experience" described in the first movement of the poem. That experience occurs in the miniscule chapel at Little Gidding, where Nicholas Ferrar and his mother had established a family "convent" in 1625. There, in the troubled seventeenth century, at a place known for its homely but profound piety, a place known and revered by George Herbert and visited by King Charles I, prayer dominated the round of daily life. The Prayer Book offices and the canonical hours sanctified time through the night hours as well as through the busy days, and provided a setting where the "intersection of time by timelessness" was constant. In this poem, the chapel of Little Gidding is a symbol for the Church both as it should be and as it essentially is, the home one comes to at the end. Then, too, this final poem represents an experience of the Holy Spirit in prayer. Thus the image of fire, at the same time destructive and potentially cleansing and purgative, is seen finally as the fire of Whitsun or Pentecost, God's spirit, divine love

47

freeing us from the limitations of desire to enter ever more fully into communion with God.

The opening lines of the first movement constitute an intense poetic expression of the experience encountered by Eliot in the chapel at Little Gidding. The time is "midwinter spring," a peculiar season, eternal and apparently suspended in time, when in the short day the sun shines but does not heat; it shines so brightly that it seems to flame the ice with a "windless cold that is the heart's heat." And yet that windless cold is inwardly perceived to be as warm as fire. The light has now become fire, fire that warms and stirs the dumb spirit. It is the fire of Pentecost. The Holy Spirit flares in the dark time of the year, in the wintertime of life when hope fades. "Between melting and freezing/ The soul's sap quivers"—the promise is received and understood and new life begins. The poet knows that this event taking place at Little Gidding, anywhere and nowhere, is not of this temporal order in which we are enchained. It takes place at the intersection of time and eternity, both in and out of time, at spring time and beyond time.

Whatever happened to Eliot at Little Gidding, it surely involved something so deeply felt that words fail. The experience can only be expressed imperfectly here through images both vibrant and startling, and yet images derived from tradition, the metaphysical tradition of the seventeenth century to which Eliot was heir. In all likelihood the experience at Little Gidding occurred in the context of prayer, while the poet knelt

> Where prayer has been valid. . . .
> And what the dead had no speech for, when living,
> They can tell you, being dead: the communication
> Of the dead is tongued with fire beyond the language
> of the living.

> Here, the intersection of the timeless moment
> Is England and nowhere. Never and always.

It would seem, furthermore, that the experience was associated
with corporate worship, specifically with the ritual of Holy
Saturday found in the Anglican Missal, with its blessing of the
new fire and with its prayer to God "that we may be enkindled
by thy light and enlightened with the fire of thy brightness,"
that God will truly "enlighten our hearts and understandings,
that we may be found worthy to attain unto the light of everlasting life." To take this seriously is to believe and, believing thus,
to engage in that meeting at the intersection of time and eternity
which nourishes the soul and dresses it for eternal life.

Eliot here seems to have in mind that image of the Holy Spirit
as tongues of fire which Henry Vaughan uses when he writes:
"Thou art/ Refining fire, O then refine my heart,/ My foul, foul
heart! Thou art immortall heat,/ Heat motion gives; Then warm it,
till it beat." Acknowledging that in this first movement of "Little
Gidding" Eliot is making direct reference to the Holy Spirit,
symbolized by purgatorial fire, the critic Audrey Cahill enlarges
upon the biblical images suggested by Eliot's inclusion of the fire
motif as one of his images of light. Fire, she reminds us,

> is associated with the holiness of God (Exod. 3:2), with purga-
> tion by God (Isa. 6:6-7), with the inspiration of God (Ps.
> 39:3), with the baptism of the Spirit (Luke 3:16), and with
> the power of God (I Kings 18:38, Acts 2:4). That this experi-
> ence is set in midwinter, in frost and ice, is a reminder of the
> painful paradox suggested in East Coker II:

> > If to be warmed, then I must freeze
> > And quake in frigid purgatorial fires
> > Of which the flame is roses, and the smoke is briars.[24]

The fire symbol meant all of this to Eliot and more. It suggests
also the idea of "the constant flux which underlies all natural
processes" in the philosophy of Heraclitus, as well as the fire

sermon of Buddha. Its emphasis on "the destructive agony of the senses" is related to the Christian understanding of purgatorial fire.[25]

The lyrics opening the second movement of each *Quartet* provide a music and a meaning of their own. In "Burnt Norton" the eternal order is depicted; in "East Coker," the actual disorder of the world as experienced by the poet is vividly portrayed. "The Dry Salvages" dwells on the ceaseless progress of death, destruction, and decay, pointing at the end to the Annunciation and the hope it represents. In "Little Gidding" we are again confronted by the grim reality of our earthly existence, a reality dramatically reinforced for Eliot by the devastation of war and, in particular, the bombing of London. The death of people and of the fruits of their labors in the modern industrial society forces us to realize that all we cherish most will perish, if it has not already. The destruction of life and of civilization is described in this part of the poem as the triumph of the four elements (each prominent in one of the *Four Quartets*) over those who thought they could control them. The language of the poet is disturbingly effective:

> There are flood and drouth
> Over the eyes and in the mouth. . . .
> The parched eviscerate soil
> Gapes at the vanity of toil,
> Laughs without mirth.
> This is the death of earth.

Here Eliot is a prophet warning the civilization he respects and would perpetuate, warning it of the doom that shall surely come unless its people turn and repent, surrendering their prideful lives to the doing of God's will and to the promotion of love and peace. At the end of the poem he appears to be saying that the present

50

chaos and destruction have resulted from our neglect, denial, and ignorance of the foundation of this civilization, that of a people born of and nurtured by the Christian faith. In the three stanzas beginning

> Water and fire succeed
> The town, the pasture and the weed

down to "This is the death of water and fire," Eliot focuses our attention on the power of air, earth, water, and fire over all that is temporal and physical. Things man-made have been annihilated and drawn back into the four elements; it is a negative vision. According to Bergsten, furthermore, these three stanzas "sum up the previous *Quartets* by recapitulation of significant images. There are the roses and the 'Dust in the air suspended' of *Burnt Norton* I, the 'wall, the wainscot and the mouse' from *East Coker* I, the images of water from *The Dry Salvages* and the 'sanctuary and choir' reminiscent of the chapel of *Little Gidding*."[26]

Eliot then turns to the past, to the High Middle Ages when the faith was lively and civilization in process of maturing. For the rest of the second movement he chooses to imitate Dante's *terza rima*, the rhyme scheme used in *The Divine Comedy* (that is, aba, bcb, cdc, and so forth). He does this, difficult and awkward as it is, because he wants to make connection with "the marred foundations we forgot,/ Of sanctuary and choir." The three-part rhyme scheme itself represents the "foundations," symbolizing as it does the Holy Trinity, Father, Son, and Holy Spirit. With this in mind the poet in this passage remembers his experience as a fire warden in London during the blitz. He tells of his encounter one night with "a familiar compound ghost" with whom he holds a conversation. The lines have a familiar ring to anyone acquainted with Dante's *Inferno*, for they are reminiscent of that poet's encounters with ghosts and spirits of the past, particularly the meeting with his tutor, Brunetto Latini. Eliot does not identify the ghost, which is compounded of all the dead poets who have become a part of Eliot's *persona* now. And it is the poet himself engaged upon an introspective self-assessment. Most importantly, the

51

reader must understand that Eliot is present in both persons of the conversation. In the course of that conversation the poet reveals that he roams between two worlds, finding

> words I never thought to speak
> In streets I never thought I should revisit
> When I left my body on a distant shore.

The end of the roaming is in the discovery that his life is finally and inescapably hopeless until it has been renewed in the cleansing and purgatorial fire. Again Eliot gives us echoes of Dante; here, the image of Arnaut Daniel, the Provencal poet Dante encounters among the lustful in Purgatory, who "hid himself within the fire" and thus was brought into the dance, the dance of love.

The third movement of "Little Gidding" begins with a warning against indifference and against lapsing into old age and infirmity. Over against indifference Eliot places memory, which liberates us from imprisonment in time and frees us for the expansion of our desire into love. The use of memory (*anamnesis*) is for the purpose of liberation, so that we may perceive divine purpose revealed in and through profane ecstasy. The liberation is also to a state of detachment comparable to the openness, or 'availability,' that I have previously discussed. For it is by grace that the divine love is perceived in the profane ecstasy, and grace cannot work where the self is imprisoned, enchained by itself in itself.

What is true of personal existence is also true of history, and affects the way we perceive the past. Eliot, detached from servitude to past or future, perceives the underlying unity among those who have been in opposition in the civil wars of the seventeenth century and always. Opposites are united by the harmony of underlying intentions, the pursuit of holiness, the quest for love, the endless struggle for spiritual values—such idealistic goals as always seem to end in defeat. Laudians and Puritans in the seventeenth century, both pursuing holiness although otherwise opposed, labored, as those like them labor now, with the conviction eloquently expressed by Dame Julian of Norwich in her fourteenth-century *Showings*, "All shall be well and all manner of things shall be well."

When we regard history from the perspective of the still point, or in the light of the Incarnation, we perceive that the really important events concern those now dead who kept on trying, striving for holiness, claiming at times precarious victories but always in the end apparently defeated. Yet they have followed Christ and, as they journeyed, desire has been transformed into love.

The fourth movement of "Little Gidding" opens with another, climactic lyric, the image of a fighter plane:

> The dove descending breaks the air
> With flame of incandescent terror. . . .
> The only hope, or else despair
>   Lies in the choice of pyre or pyre—
>   To be redeemed from fire by fire.

As the lyric opens the image of the fighter-bomber of World War II is evoked, spitting its fire, its rain of death, the "incandescent terror." The words themselves snap and crack, hitting out at us, as with "*d*ove *d*escending" and "incan*d*escent *t*error." Then the initial image of the fighter plane is expanded and transformed. The dove which is the bomber becomes the dove of the Holy Spirit and the flames that were destructive become purgative. These stanzas become an observance of the day of Pentecost. The deadly tongues of flame become the tongues of Pentecost and "the communication of the dead . . . tongued with fire beyond the

53

language of the living." These tongues proclaim not death but salvation, declaring the possibility of liberation from sin and error.

The transformation from death to renewing grace is not, however, as abrupt as we may think at first glance. The Heraclitean dictum that the way down is the way up still holds. Paradoxically, the image of the death-dealing dove prepares the way for the life-giving dove by confronting us with our sin and error, with the possible obliteration of the self and of civilization. It reveals our fragility and our finitude and thus humbles and opens us, making us accessible to the working of the Holy Spirit.

Salvation is God's doing. The merciful God judges us and reaches out to save us by the power of the Holy Spirit. But just as Mary at the Annunciation was required to give herself over to God's grace, surrendering self-will, so we must accede to the working of the life-giving Spirit in us. We must choose one or the other, "pyre or pyre," choose one way or the other out of our personal and social hells. Both pyres are redemptive in the sense that both save us from enchainment in meaningless time. Both ways involve pain and torment such as prompt us to ask who "devised" them.

The answer is clear. It is love working, beckoning us on, leading us through the fire, fire that torments and refines in painful trials. It is love, the wounded surgeon, who endured the fire on our behalf and provides the fire that energizes us with the divine Spirit to begin again, to live anew and thus to join the dance at the still point, participants in eternal life. The lyric emphasizes the Holy Spirit as the vital agent, the ground of meeting, whereby the eternal intervenes in the temporal—judging, purging, and energizing. And yet the poem clearly implies that the Spirit's work is only possible when we surrender ourselves with Mary, saying, "Be it unto me according to thy will."

The final movement of "Little Gidding" draws all together

in a kind of musical climax of considerable complexity. The movement is also an affirmation of the poet's faith. The first three lines recall the hypothesis concerning time with which "Burnt Norton" begins, as well as the central theme of "East Coker" presented in the opening and closing lines derived from the motto of Mary, Queen of Scots, "In my beginning is my end. . . . In my end is my beginning." In the *Quartets* the poet moves from the quest for his origins to the conviction that his death is a new beginning. In a sense the key word is "end," interpreted not only as death but as "telos," purpose.

Derek Traversi writes, "If the final achievement of *consciousness* lies . . . in the recognition of a final reality outside the process of temporal sequence, the end to which our lives are directed . . . is in fact 'where we start from.' "[27] This is true of the poetic process and of human existence. Any action, whether it involve death or pilgrimage, or some combination of the two, provides us with a new beginning. This is so because we must die to selfishness, self-centeredness, aware of our finitude, before we can grow. "East Coker" reads "In order to possess what you do not possess/ You must go by the way of dispossession." Here we read, "We die with the dying. . . . We are born with the dead." The lines echo St. Paul's Christ mysticism and remind us of the theology of baptism; in that initiatory sacrament, we die and rise again with Christ. On another level we die with the dead, entering into the communion of the saints, and are henceforth united with them, returning with them, participants in the "communication . . . tongued with fire, beyond the language of the living." Participants in eternity, we perceive with an intense consciousness that disparate occasions, mystic ecstasy, and death are all moments when eternity intersects time. "The moment of the rose and the moment of the yew-tree/ Are of equal duration"; that is, both are beyond duration in the temporal sense. The rose and the yew-tree stand for life, generation, affirmation, passion, and desire as well as for mystic ecstasy and death, the *via negativa,* new birth through death, the two symbols joined finally in the love that is their souce and their fulfillment.

To understand that the realities of life and of death are equally momentous because implicit in every moment, one must perceive the meaning, Eliot tells us in "The Dry Salvages," of many generations. We cannot understand or redeem time unless we are conscious of the *kairoi*, or significant times, through history. Chronological time, ordinary history, is but a string of meaningless events unless transformed into saving history. And such holy history is perceived first at the still point where eternity intersects time, the timeless moments, annunciations born of the one Annunciation. This holy history *is* history: the rest is illusion, enchained in time and doomed to oblivion. Thus in the chapel at Little Gidding, where the poet prays on his knees and through prayer participates in the meaningful *kairos* born of the one *Kairos*, Jesus Christ, all significant history is present and potent. Indeed, at any moment in time in the Christian life, all significant history is present as the combination of all moments. Potentially, then, every moment is an annunciation after the pattern of the one Annunciation, hidden from us by our lack of consciousness. There is here a sense of holiness concentrated beyond imagination into holy love.

The final section of this last movement draws together in a remarkable way symbols from all of the preceding poems. These symbols or images are now presented as transformed through the experiences narrated in the course of the sequence. Furthermore, they are now subordinated to a significant order. In the final stanza the poem comes full circle and, Eliot tells us, the purpose and end of all our voyaging in life is to return to the place from which we began. We must return to the fragile, fleeting moments, the dim, illusive *kairoi* at which eternity intercepted time, and perceive the true meaning of those experiences. Through the gate leading to the rose garden, the gate leading the voyager through all there is to discover, is the gate leading to "the last of earth left to discover," the significant soil which is the beginning, the source of life, and the key to ultimate meaning. At the source of the river of time, at the still point, there is "the voice of the hidden waterfall/ And the children in the apple-tree," hints and guesses dimly perceived, and there is the stillness "between two waves of the sea." In the stillness all is restored, transformed, and fulfilled.

This is the end and purpose of our voyaging and the cost is known: the cost is not less than everything and it involves, finally, self-surrender. Such renunciation leads to victory over death, sin, and meaninglessness, as in Dame Julian's "And all shall be well and all manner of thing shall be well."

The poet is mindful of the consummation, "When the tongues of flame are all in-folded/ Into the crowned knot of fire." Then are all opposites united, transformed in the lover's knot. Rose garden and chapel, desire and love, nature and grace, are seen at last in their true relationship, a vital and creative unity. Here indeed the fire transforms the rose, symbolizing the unity of mortality and immortality, so that it becomes the rose of heaven and symbol of the resurrection. Once more there is an intimation of Dante and his vision of "all things in a single volume bound by Love," at the close of the *Paradiso*.

The vision at the end does not mean that we have in some way arrived at the final terminus and that we can stop exploring. It means, rather, that we must fare forward. Our imperfect experiences of reality, imperfectly expressed in words, are drawn forth by and ever lead toward the Love that draws us into the dance at the still point and transfigures all into that which is for us, finally, inexpressible.

vi. IN CONCLUSION

The unity of these poems has been viewed in diverse ways by diverse people. The *Four Quartets* can be understood as representing the different seasons of the year, beginning with spring and "Burnt Norton." Each *Quartet* seems to be identified with one of the four elements: air ("Burnt Norton"), earth ("East Coker"), water ("The Dry Salvages"), and fire ("Little Gidding"). Their structure and meaning have been analyzed in relation to the musical quartet and the allegorical interpretation of Scripture and other literature. All interpretations are helpful and tend to emphasize both the unity and the richness of the poems.[28]

Throughout I have emphasized the lyrical fourth movement of each of the quartets because I believe that these sections represent the key and the heart of the entire sequence. By analyzing them, it is possible to discern an order and a progression. In "Burnt Norton" the poet is concerned with natural religion or general revelation, and with moments of illumination such as happen to anyone, which require only faith at the moment of revelation. This constitutes the necessary beginning; it is the place from which we all start in this life. Here the dominant image is air. In "East Coker," where the element emphasized is earth, our attention is focused on the Atonement through the passion of Christ, the wounded surgeon. He dies that we may die and live.

In "The Dry Salvages" the poet is concerned with water and with the Annunciation, and thus with the Incarnation, the intersection of time by eternity. The Annunciation proves not only a witness to that intersection, but a pattern for response to it. It also provides meaning for understanding "hints and guesses," the fleeting moments of illumination which are the focus in the first quartet. But the chief lesson we learn is that in order to receive revelation, it is necessary that we submit ourselves to it in faith, as did the Virgin Mary, the daughter of her Son. Finally, in "Little Gidding" we are concerned with fire and the Holy Spirit, God's love as a purifying, refining, energizing power. In the end there is revealed what was only dimly and inadequately perceived

59

in earlier moments of intense consciousness, in the rose garden and elsewhere. This is Pentecost and the faith of the Church born there and then, providing that holy routine, "prayer, observance, discipline, thought and action," whereby we are enabled to participate in the divine not only in rare moments but steadily, regularly, although still imperfectly.

Whether fully conscious of the fact or not, Eliot seems to have here the right order for our time. For we ourselves begin with hints and guesses. Then, conscious of all that threatens our existence (death, sin, and meaninglessness), we discover the mercy of God shown through the passion of his Son on the cross. We discover, that is, the high priest who is himself the sacrifice in order that God's true nature as sacrificial love may be known and that we may be born anew to lives of sacrificial love. It is only then, after we have known God's mercy, that we are capable of recognizing that the sacrificial lamb is divine and that his mother is indeed the daughter of her son. Then all annunciations are made clear and the intersection of time by eternity is revealed and ordinary existence gains significance. Thus liberated by sacrificial love and responding to that love in the spirit of the one Annunciation, we become aware of the activity of the Holy Spirit, the purifying fire which has been at work in us from the beginning. The Holy Spirit is recognized as the ground of meeting. It gives meaning to all social relationships whereby we become more fully human as individuals.

Furthermore, although we are led to conclude that our progress is from inadequate perceptions of reality on the ordinary plane of natural theology in "Burnt Norton" to a perception of reality that takes place within the context of the Church and its teachings, Eliot had this conclusion in mind before he began the first poem. Ever since his conversion and reception into the Church of England in 1927 Eliot had been a practicing churchman, and lived for the rest of his life in the context of prayer book worship. His mature faith, furthermore, was formed under the influence of such Anglican divines as Lancelot Andrewes, Richard Hooker, John Donne, and George Herbert. The sermons of Lancelot Andrewes Eliot regarded as literary monuments of immense value, fruits of the English Church's influence on both intellect and sensibility. From Hooker and Andrewes Eliot gained much insight into the richness of divine revelation and the process whereby Christians participate in it.[29] Both divines emphasized the coherence of nature and grace, of natural and revealed theology, and both focused on the doctrine of the Incarnation as the key to that coherence. Both Hooker and Andrewes emphasized the richness and wholeness of divine revelation over against the Puritans, who seemed to set nature and grace in separate compartments and in opposition to each other.

Prior to the publication of the first *Quartet*, "Burnt Norton," Eliot had produced a full-blown theology in the seventh of the *Choruses from "The Rock."* He begins with the creation by God and describes the agonizing quest for God in the primitive religions, on through the "Higher Religions," to the Incarnation. Eliot's *Four Quartets* concern this struggle towards God and thus towards meaningful human existence. The main point is that there is a reality, that this reality is personal, that it is love as revealed in Jesus Christ. We only dimly perceive this reality and are often led astray into illusions, but we keep struggling in the knowledge that the key to the struggle lies in the waiting. Through the waiting, refraining from imposing false patterns of our own devising, we become available, open to receive the pattern offered to us. The *Four Quartets* involve the poet's attempt to communicate the gospel, reminding us of what we have forgotten in ways that modern humans can understand, using images other than the timeworn traditional ones, and evoking responses as if to something novel and unfamiliar. Such was Eliot's vocation, the Christian poet composing words in patterns that in themselves yield to the divine pattern and become vehicles of salvation.

In writing this study I have found Helen Gardner's *The Composition of Four Quartets* particularly valuable, as well as the other critical works cited in the notes. Other useful works are Ethel Cornwall's *The Still Point* (New Brunswick, NJ: Rutgers University Press, n.d.) and Eloise Knapp Hay's *T.S. Eliot's Negative Way* (Cambridge, MA: Harvard University Press, 1982).

For biographical data on Eliot, see James E. Miller, Jr., *T.S. Eliot's Personal Waste Land: Exorcism of the Demons* (University Park and London: The Pennsylvania State University Press, 1977) and Helen Gardner's *The Composition of Four Quartets.*

For Eliot's churchmanship, see T.S. Matthew, *Great Tom: Notes Towards a Definition of T.S. Eliot* (London: Weidenfeld and Nicholson, 1974), pp. 119–20; Robert Sencourt, *T.S. Eliot* (New York: Dodd, Mead, and Co., 1971), pp. 167–8; Martin Jarrett-Kerr, " 'Of Clerical Cut': Retrospective Reflections on Eliot's Churchmanship," in *Eliot in Perspective* (New York: Humanities Press, 1970), pp. 233–51.

For Eliot and Vorticism, see Timothy Materer's *Vortex: Pound, Eliot, and Lewis* (Ithaca, NY and London: Cornell University Press, 1979).

1. Steffan Bergsten, *Time and Eternity: A Study in the Structure and Symbolism of T.S. Eliot's Four Quartets* (Stockholm: Svenska Bokforlaget, 1960), p. 125.
2. Richard Wollheim, *F.H. Bradley*, p. 47, cited in Peter G. Ellis, "T.S. Eliot, F.H. Bradley, and 'Four Quartets,' " *Research Studies* 37:2, p. 94.
3. Ibid., p. 98.
4. R.L. Brett, "Mysticism and Incarnation in *Four Quartets*," *English* 16:98-99.
5. Helen Gardner, *The Composition of Four Quartets* (London and Boston: Faber and Faber, 1978), p. 38.
6. William T. Moynihan, "Character and Action in *Four Quartets*," in *T.S. Eliot*, ed. Linda W. Wagner (New York: McGraw-Hill, n.d.), p. 84.
7. *Composition*, p. 83.
8. Derek Traversi, *T.S. Eliot: The Longer Poems* (New York and London: Harcourt, Brace, Jovanovich, 1976), p. 108.
9. Bergsten, p. 182.
10. Moynihan, p. 88.
11. Mollie Panter-Downes, *London War Notes 1935-1945* (New York: Farrar, Straus & Giroux, 1971), p. 41.
12. David Ward, *T.S. Eliot Between Two Worlds* (London and Boston: Routledge and Kegan Paul, 1973), p. 242.
13. Traversi, pp. 134-5.
14. Richard Hooker, *Works* (7th Keble ed.), 3:606-615; Lancelot Andrewes, *Ninety-Six Sermons* (Library of Anglo-Catholic Theology), 2:342; Gabriel Marcel, *Foi et Realité* (Aubier: Éditions Montaigne, 1967), p. 125.
15. *Composition*, p. 109.
16. Traversi, p. 147.
17. Helen Gardner, *The Art of T.S. Eliot* (New York: E.P. Dutton, 1959), pp. 169-70.
18. Panter-Downes, p. 133.
19. *The Art*, pp. 171-2.

20. John V. Taylor, *The Go-Between God* (London: SCM Press, 1972), p. 17.
21. Audrey Cahill, *T.S. Eliot: The Human Predicament* (Natal: University of Natal Press, 1967), p. 177.
22. Ibid., pp. 181-2.
23. T.S. Eliot, *Murder in the Cathedral,* in *The Complete Poems and Plays* (New York: Harcourt, Brace and Company, 1952), p. 221.
24. Cahill, pp. 189-90.
25. Ward, pp. 264-5.
26. Bergsten, p. 236.
27. Traversi, p. 210.
28. See Cahill's diagram of the *Quartets* illustrating their unity, pp. 212-215. See also R.P. Blackmur's analysis in "Unappeasable and Peregrine: Behavior and the Four Quartets" in *Thought* 26 (spring 1951): 59-60. See also Gardner's discussion in *The Art of T.S. Eliot.*
29. See Eliot's essay, "Lancelot Andrewes," in *Selected Prose of T.S. Eliot*, ed. Frank Kermode (New York: Harcourt, Brace, Jovanovich, 1975), especially pp. 180-1.